STANDING T

Standing To

U. A. FANTHORPE

HARRY CHAMBERS/PETERLOO POETS

First published in 1982
by Harry Chambers/Peterloo Poets
Treovis Farm Cottage, Upton Cross, Liskeard, Cornwall PL14 5BQ

Second impression 1985

ISBN 0 905291 35 2

Printed in Great Britain by
Latimer Trend & Company Ltd, Plymouth

ACKNOWLEDGEMENTS are due to the editors of the following journals and anthologies: *Arvon Foundation Poetry Competition 1980 Anthology*, *Bananas*, *Country Life*, *Encounter*, *Gloucestershire & Avon Life*, *London Lines*, *Mandeville Press*, *Meridian*, *P.N. Review*, *New Poetry* (ed. Norman Hidden), *New Poetry 3* (Arts Council, 1977), *New Poetry 4* (Arts Council, 1978), *New Poetry 6* (Arts Council, 1980), *Observer*, *Poetry Review*, *Quarto*, *South West Review*, *Times Literary Supplement*, *Tribune*.

Several of the poems in the section *Christmas Cards* first appeared in *Poems for Christmas* (Peterloo, 1981).

'Four Dogs' was first published in a limited edition of 250 by Treovis Press.

'Rising Damp' won 3rd prize in the 1980 Arvon Foundation Poetry Competition.

'Sisyphus' won 1st prize in the 1981 *New Poetry* Competition.

Some of these poems have been read on *Poetry Now* (BBC Radio 3) and others on *Books, Plays, Poems* (BBC Radio 4, VHF for Schools).

Cover drawing: 'Caporal Maurice Empereur of the Chasseurs Alpins on Guard in the Little St Bernard's Pass at Seez, Tarantaize, France' by Anthony Gross, R.A. (Courtesy of the Trustees of The Imperial War Museum.)

Harry Chambers/Peterloo Poets receives financial assistance from The Arts Council of Great Britain.

For Rosemarie Bailey

Contents

STATIONS UNDERGROUND

Horace: Odes I, no. XXIV

durum: sed levius fit patientia
Quidquid corrigere est nefas.

Loss hurts. Yet patience helps us to endure
The ills no human should presume to cure.

(tr. James Michie)

Fanfare

For Winifrid Fanthorpe, born 5th February 1895, died 13th November 1978.

You, in the old photographs, are always
The one with the melancholy half-smile, the one
Who couldn't quite relax into the joke.

My extrovert dog of a father,
With his ragtime blazer and his swimming togs
Tucked like a swiss roll under his arm,
Strides in his youth towards us down some esplanade,

Happy as Larry. You, on his other arm,
Are anxious about the weather forecast,
His overdraft, or early closing day.

You were good at predicting failure: marriages
Turned out wrong because you said they would.
You knew the rotations of armistice and war,
Watched politicians' fates with gloomy approval.

All your life you lived in a minefield,
And were pleased, in a quiet way, when mines
Exploded. You never actually said
I told you so, but we could tell you meant it.

Crisis was your element. You kept your funny stories,
Your music-hall songs for doodlebug and blitz-nights.
In the next cubicle, after a car-crash, I heard you
Amusing the nurses with your trench wit through the blood.

Magic alerted you. Green, knives and ladders
Will always scare me through your tabus.
Your nightmare was Christmas; so much organised
Compulsory whoopee to be got through.

You always had some strategem for making
Happiness keep its distance. Disaster
Was what you planned for. You always
Had hoarded loaves or candles up your sleeve.

Houses crumbled around your ears, taps leaked,
Electric light bulbs went out all over England,
Because for you homes were only provisional,
Bivouacs on the stony mountain of living.

You were best at friendship with chars, gipsies,
Or very far-off foreigners. Well-meaning neighbours
Were dangerous because they lived near.

Me too you managed best at a distance. On the landline
From your dugout to mine, your nightly
Pass, friend was really often quite jovial.

You were the lonely figure in the doorway
Waving goodbye in the cold, going back to a sink-full
Of crockery dirtied by those you loved. We
Left you behind to deal with our crusts and gristle.

I know why you chose now to die. You foresaw
Us approaching the Delectable Mountains,
And didn't feel up to all the cheers and mafficking.

But how, dearest, will even you retain your
Special brand of hard-bitten stoicism
Among the halleluyas of the triumphant dead?

Four Dogs

1. CERBERUS

The first was known simply
As *the dog*. Later writers gave him a name,
Three heads, a collar of serpents,
And a weakness for cake.
They also claimed he could be
Calmed by magic, charmed by music,
And even, on one occasion, thrashed.

Later writers can seldom be trusted.
Primary sources are more reliable:
This dog guarded his master's gate,
Wagged his ears and tail at visitors,
Admitted them all, and saw to it
That nobody ever got out.

2. ANUBIS

The civil Egyptians made
Their dog half man. The dog end
Had the usual doggy tastes
For digging, and bones. But the human half
Was drawn to conservation and chemistry,
Liked pickling, preserving, dissecting,
Distillation; added artistry
To the dog's enthusiasm. Undertaking
Became Egyptian art.

3. EL PERRO (GOYA)

There was a man who never blinked.
Helmeted in deafness, he set down
What he saw: the unembarrassed beastliness
Of humanity, country picnics, rape,
Blank-faced politicians, idiot obstinate kings,
Famine, firing-squads, milkmaids.
He charted nightmare's dominion
On his house's walls. To him appeared
The thing itself, snouting its way
Up from underground. He drew it
As it was: darkness, a dog's head,
Mild, mongrel, appalling.

4. SHANDY

The fourth dog lives in my house with me
Like a sister, loves me doggedly,
Guiltily, abstractedly; disobeys me
When I am not looking. I love her
Abstractedly, guiltily; feed her; try
Not to let her know she reminds me
Of the other dogs.

At the Ferry

Laconic as anglers and, like them, submissive,
The grey-faced loiterers on the bank,
Charon, of your river.

They are waiting their turn. Nothing we do
Distracts them much. It was you, Charon, I saw,
Refracted in a woman's eyes.

Patient, she sat in a wheelchair,
In an X-ray department, waiting for someone
To do something to her,

Given a magazine, folded back
At the problem page: *What should I do*
About my husband's impotence?

Is a registry office marriage
Second-best? I suffer from a worrying
Discharge from my vagina.

In her hands she held the thing obediently;
Obediently moved her eyes in the direction
Of the problems of the restless living.

But her mind deferred to another dimension.
Outward bound, tenderly inattentive, she was waiting,
Charon, for you.

And the nineteen-stone strong man, felled
By his spawning brain, lying still to the sound
Of the DJ's brisk chirrup;

He wasn't listening, either. He was on the lookout
For the flurry of water as your craft
Comes about in the current.

I saw you once, boatman, lean by your punt-pole
On an Oxford river, in the dubious light
Between willow and water,

Where I had been young and lonely, being
Now loved, and older; saw you in the tender, reflective
Gaze of the living

Looking down at me, deliberate,
And strange in the half-light, saying nothing,
Claiming me, Charon, for life.

Rising Damp

(for C.A.K. and R.K.M.)

'A river can sometimes be diverted, but it is a very hard thing to lose it altogether.'
(J. G. Head: *paper read to the Auctioneers' Institute in 1907*)

At our feet they lie low,
The little fervent underground
Rivers of London

Effra, Graveney, Falcon, Quaggy,
Wandle, Walbrook, Tyburn, Fleet

Whose names are disfigured,
Frayed, effaced.

These are the Magogs that chewed the clay
To the basin that London nestles in.
These are the currents that chiselled the city,
That washed the clothes and turned the mills,
Where children drank and salmon swam
And wells were holy.

They have gone under.
Boxed, like the magician's assistant.
Buried alive in earth.
Forgotten, like the dead.

They return spectrally after heavy rain,
Confounding suburban gardens. They infiltrate
Chronic bronchitis statistics. A silken
Slur haunts dwellings by shrouded
Watercourses, and is taken
For the footing of the dead.

Being of our world, they will return
(Westbourne, caged at Sloane Square,
Will jack from his box),
Will deluge cellars, detonate manholes,
Plant effluent on our faces,
Sink the city.

Effra, Graveney, Falcon, Quaggy,
Wandle, Walbrook, Tyburn, Fleet

It is the other rivers that lie
Lower, that touch us only in dreams
That never surface. We feel their tug
As a dowser's rod bends to the source below

Phlegethon, Acheron, Lethe, Styx.

Sisyphus

'The struggla itself towards the heights is enough to fill a man's heart. One must imagine Sisyphus happy.'
(Camus: *The Myth of Sisyphus*)

Apparently I rank as one
Of the more noteworthy sights down here.
As to that, I can't judge, having
No time to spare for tourists.

My preoccupations are this stone
And this hill. I have to push
The one up the other.

A trivial task for a team, an engine,
A pair of horses. The interest lies
Not in the difficulty of the doing,

But the difficulty for the doer. I accept this
As my vocation: to do what I cannot do.
The stone and I are

Close. I know its every wart, its ribby ridges,
Its snags, its lips. And the stone knows me,
Cheek, chin and shoulders, elbow, groin, shin, toe,
Muscle, bone, cartilage and muddied skinprint,
My surfaces, my angles and my levers.

The hill I know by heart too,
Have studied incline, foothold, grain,
With watchmaker's patience.

Concentration is mutual. The hill
Is hostile to the stone and me.
The stone resents me and the hill.

But I am the mover. I cannot afford
To spend energy on emotion. I push
The stone up the hill. At the top

It falls, and I pursue it,
To heave it up again. Time not spent
On doing this is squandered time.

The gods must have had a reason
For setting me this task. I have forgotten it,
And I do not care.

The Guide

The level-headed Greeks grasped
Their underworld, and charted it. Rivers,
Hills and dry land behaved
Geographically, appropriately. Sentence
Was passed by a panel
Of High Court Judges, with an assessor
To help with hard cases,
And the terrain, being logical,
Enforced the law.

Dante the bureaucrat invented
A new filing system for
The irregular dead, pigeon-holing them
As pertinently as the Mikado.
They fluttered and squeaked,
But he netted and mounted them,
Steady as Aristotle, knowing
The unutterable articulations of peace,
From purgatory to paradise, were based
On the accurate taxonomy of sin.

Dispossession, and the secrets
Of his beemaster father,
Taught Vergil more than men know.
He trudged further into suffering
And pity than other people,
Led to accept his vocation
By the annals of the hive. He knew
How drones die nobly
In midsummer air after mating,
Or sombrely, autumnal offerings;
How the workforce fly their wings
To rags, to death; how virgin knights
Are stabbed in their royal cradles;
How tired and failing monarchs
Undertake forced marches upcountry

To found new colonies. He knew
That the bees' god is the Future,
Which consumes first the loving,
The wise, the beautiful, the brave,
Because they are special, and favours
The ordinary bee, the bee-in-the-air,
Aeneas, the survivor.
So Orpheus has to die. So Rome
Goes on, as Vergil knew it would,
Monumentally second-rate city.

About Hell, too, he knew more
Than the others. Through blunt-edged Latin,
Its meanings scuffed by ages of misuse,
He found ways of wording the unsayable,
Fathomed echo-chambers behind the dulled
And vague, and told us:
Hell is a sort of underground bog.
There are no landmarks. In it
Those we have loved and failed
Turn their backs for ever.

The Passing of Alfred

'He (Tennyson) died with his hand on his Shakespeare, and the moon shining full into the window over him . . . A worthy end.'
(Queen Victoria: *Journal*)

Our fathers were good at dying.
They did it lingeringly,
As if they liked it; correctly,
With earnest attention to detail,
Codicils brought up to date,
Forgiveness, confession, last-gasp
Penitence properly witnessed
By responsible persons. Attorneys,
Clerics, physicians, all knew their place
In the civil pavane of dying.

Households discharged
Their methodical duties: said farewell
In order of precedence, outdoor staff first,
Faithful hounds respectfully mourning,
Lastly the widow-to-be, already
Pondering a transformed wardrobe.

They died in the houses,
The beds they were born in,
They died where they lived, between
Known sheets, to the obbligato
Of familiar creaks and ticks.

We who differ, whose dears are absorbed
Into breezy wards for routine terminations,
Envy our fathers their decorous endings
In error. Nothing makes extinction easy.
They also died appallingly, over
The family breakfast-cups; bloodily
In childbed; graveyard coughed themselves
Into coffins; declined from heart-break

And hunger. And however resigned,
Orderly, chaste, aesthetic the passing of Alfred,
Remorse, regret still shadowed the living after.

Like us they ran from habit to tell good news
To dead ears; like us they dreamed
Of childhood, and being forgiven;
And the dead followed them, as they do us,
Tenderly through darkness,
But fade when we turn to look in the upper air.

AFTER-EFFECTS

The Conductor

I am the conductor. I preside
Over the players, clothed in the swagger
Of my office. My imperative hands
Ordain volume and tempo. I am
The music's master.

This is the music, propped open before me:
Immense Unfinished Symphony of life,
Its intervals, blunt naturals and fugues,
Its resolutions, syncopations, shakes,
Scored for my players.

These are the players. (Stand up, friends,
And make your bows.) A random lot,
Amateurs all, for nothing at all disbars,
And finally all find parts that fit them
For my orchestra.

Listen! an excerpt: today's programme.
First subject, in flute's paediatric whine,
Transposed now to the key of senility,
Dribbling urine and spittle, difficult heartbeats
Plucking like harpstrings.

Each virtuoso has his own variation:
Depression's largo, schizophrenia's scherzo,
Mute music of the withdrawn, epileptic cadenzas,
The plagal cadence of the stretcher-borne dying,
Drum taps of the blind.

Listen again. The second subject
Is harder to hear, is sensed at last
In pauses, breves, a *did-not-come*, a rest,
A silence. For this symphony's name
Is also Farewell,

And as each player reaches his part's end
He tucks his instrument decently under his arm,
Snuffs out his candle, tiptoes demurely away
Into the dark and the stillness. For him
The concert's over.

I, the receptionist, must also play
My part, and go. I shoot my cuffs,
And watch my hectoring fingers, like the rest,
Sprout into rattlebones. And see
A new conductor,

Young, fetching, shifty, immortal,
Hermes bringer of dreams, the light-fingered,
Hermes who leads men's souls in another direction
From our world of unholy living
And wholly dying.

Inside

Inside our coloured, brisk world,
Like a bone inside a leg, lies
The world of the negative.

It is the same world, only somehow
Conviction has dribbled out of it,
Like stuffing from a toy.

A world of hypnotic clocks and unfinished
Goblin gestures. Nothing moves in a landscape
Fixed in hysteria's stasis.

This is the hushed network of nightmare.
You have lost touch with the sustaining
Ordinariness of things.

Suddenly the immense and venerable
Fallacies that prop the universe
Fail, the colossal flickering fabric
Which we must believe in so that it can be
Goes out.

Here malevolence is routine, the shadow
Is real and the world is shadow.
Here the happy-ever-after crumples
Into a rheumatoid hic-iacet.

Here the appalling and unexpected
Disaster is expected. Here the blood
Screams whispers to the flesh.

And here the alien wanders
Endless benighted streets where innocent households
Laugh behind blinds and believe in tomorrow
Like the milkbottles at the door.

Prolepsis

You look too young for the part,
Said the producer. *This is how we show*
Age on the stage.

She traced the firm ground round the eye,
Touching bone under. Make-up's black finger
Rehearsed what would come:

Mouth's drag, the florid swag
Of flesh round socket, cheekbone, chin.
The writing on the skin.

You wore age like a mask,
Young, bright, erect. Who could detect
Decomposition's mark?

Your new producer has a different touch
Who, like a headsman, can evoke
Death at a stroke.

You look too young for your age,
He said. *So let's pretend you're dead.*
He showed his hand

And touched your head.
One hemisphere's sure pilot faltered,
Brain's tempo altered,

One eye, arm, hand, side, leg and foot
Fell mute. We read you, dulled and stiff,
Half of Death's hieroglyph.

You will recover,
Claim you're mis-cast, demand a different role,
But we decipher
The writing on the soul.

A Gardener

Ours are a job lot
From the Funny Farm: shambling gangs
Of overgrown dwarfs, waiting
To be told what to do,

Or austere, executive Scotsmen,
Who issue crisp, instantly misunderstood orders,
Decamping before incomprehension
Becomes too obvious.

This one materialised
Pruning an abandoned rambler
With placid accuracy.

We spoke. I asked, he taught me
To know growths of different years,
How each year sets its signature on roses
Like hallmarked silver.

I asked what course he'd done.
He explained the high-flying
Resolution of rootstock, the frailty
Of patrician grafts.

Next day he described
The enormous thirst of trees,
The flow of sap that makes each sprig
Stretch itself into leaves,
And how in winter, each
Of these great drinkers shrinks
Inside its bark, thinks slow
Thoughts as the sun runs low.

Sandwich course? I suggested,
Job in municipal gardens?
A televisual career?
Why waste such talent here?

I haven't seen him since,
But I know where he's been;
Hollyhocks thoughtfully barbered
Before frost blacks their tops.

I know he's still around,
One day with kindest cuts
Dressing our shaggy borders;
Another, transplanted hydrangeas

Suddenly look at home.
Our scrubby grounds grow spruce.
Not much more left to do.
Will he start on the dwarfs next?

But he keeps clear of me.

Not Quite Right

Excuse me, staff-lady, but I feel rotten hungry and
thirsty, honest, I feel really ill. I'm very sincerely
grateful for having my life saved. I'm not a fool.
I died once. My wife saved my life with the kiss of life.
I feel rotten hungry and thirsty. Would you have such a
thing on you as a piece of chewing-gum or a sweet?
Any chance of your lovely company for a game of crib?

Not the blunt planes of the dull-minded,
The junket façade of the deranged;
Sanity's fine dry-point composed this profile.
Above it, hemispheres in disorder.

O the higher up the mulberry tree
The sweeter grows the berry.

Not the doll's strut of the retarded,
The see-saw footing of the insane;
He runs our corridors lightly, like a boy,
Left arm bent, hand signalling a corner.
He is a motorbike. OOOO oooo

O the higher up the mulberry tree
The sweeter grows the cherry.

Not the candid eyeballs of imbeciles,
Lunacy's limp and slippery pupils;
Regal the gaze of his eye from its socket
As he angles his head to chat.

O the higher up the mulberry tree
The sweeter grows the parsley.

We swap jargon. I call him lad,
Naming him too often, like a dog.
He looks with his sane eyes. He speaks.
He says nothing.

O the higher up the mulberry tree
The sweeter grows the herring.

He shuffles his thoughts' thumbed pack.
No joker ever trumps the brain's dead cells.
Yet once when, bothered by his gibberish,
I said to him: *Say something cheerful, lad,*
For goodness' sake, he looked me in the eye
Wisely, and spoke: *I've got my life, I'm alive.*
I'm not a fool.

O the higher up the mulberry tree
The sweeter grows the berry.

A funny set-up

Elderly chap in a cap,
Removed only (under protest)
For an EEG, crammed back on
Instantly, afterwards,
Being a piece of him.

Underlip protrudes in scorn.
Unmoved by rank, or the flighty
Niceties of medical etiquette.
Consultants become *that woman.*
Reverence is reserved for *Sunday*;
Not for the Nurses' sanctum.

We dare not question
What failing brings him here,
Though even lay eyes spot
His limp, his gloved left hand,
His puff belly, his pop eyes.
Armed in his own assessments
He has dismissed ours:
A funny set-up, this.

A nurse coaxes him
With pills. He consumes them slowly,
Censoriously. Lamely
We go our ways.
We have been weighed
In his cracked balance, and found wanting
What he has got.

Resuscitation Team

Arrives like a jinn, instantly,
Equipped with beards, white coats, its own smell,
And armfuls of metal and rubber.

Deploys promptly round the quiet bed
With horseplay and howls of laughter.
We, who are used to life, are surprised

At this larky resurrection. Runs
Through its box of tricks, prick, poke and biff,
While we watch, amazed. The indifferent patient

Is not amused, but carries little weight,
Being stripped and fumbled
By so many rugger-players. My first corpse,

If she is a corpse, lies there showing
Too much breast and leg. The team
Rowdily throws up the sponge, demands soap and water,

Leaves at the double. One of us,
Uncertainly, rearranges the night-dress.
Is it professional to observe the proprieties

Now of her who leaves privately
Wheeled past closed doors, her face
Still in the rictus of victory?

Lament for the Patients

These were far from lovely in their lives,
And when they died, they were instantly forgotten.

These were the permanent patients, the ones
Whose disease was living. Their trophy, death,
Being to no one's advantage, was kept dark.

These had quiet funerals (*no flowers,*
Please), silent incinerations, hushed-up autopsies;
Their dying figured in obituary columns
Of local papers only.

On these specialists had practised specialities;
Had weighed and measured; had taken samples
Of blood and urine; had tested IQs,
Reflexes, patience; had applied
Shock treatment, drugs and nice hot cups of tea.

Of these specialists had washed their hands,
Having failed to arrive at a satisfactory
Diagnosis (anglicè: having failed to infect them
With a reason for living). Therefore they died.

To me came the news of their dying:
From the police (*Was this individual*
A patient of yours?); from ambulance
Control (*Our team report this patient*
You sent us to fetch is deceased already);
From tight-lipped telephoning widowers
(*My wife died in her sleep last night*);
From carboned discharge letters (*I note*
That you have preserved the brain. We would certainly
Be very interested in this specimen);
From curt press cuttings (*Man found dead.*
Foul play not suspected). I annotated their notes
With their final symptom: *died.*
Therefore I remember them.

These I remember:
Sonia, David, Penny, who chose death.
Lynn and Gillian, who died undiagnosed.
Peter, whose death was enigmatic.
Simple Betty, who suddenly stopped living.
Lionhearted Gertrude, who persevered to the end.
Patricia, so sorry for herself,
For whom I was not sufficiently sorry.
Julian, the interesting case. Alan,
Broken by a lorry, resurrected by surgeons,
Who nevertheless contrived at length to die.

Not for these the proper ceremonies, the solemn crowds,
The stripped gun-carriage, the slow march from *Saul*,
The tumulus, the friendly possessions
At hand in the dark. Not even
The pauper's deal coffin, brief office
Of the uncared-for. Only the recital
Of disembodied voices in a clerk's ear,
A final emendation of the text.

Spring Afternoon

The doves purr in the trees. The wild inmates
Of Stoke Park Mental Hospital next door
Shout their improper comments from barred windows.

Forsythia burns. Homely wallflowers breathe out
The smell of heaven. The nurses and the patients
Are taking tea in deckchairs in the garden,

Under the trees. Depressives and obsessives
Call gaily to us as they play at croquet.
The epileptics doze off in the grass.

Caged in normality, we dumbly watch
From our dark office windows, feel that something—
Spring? or our sanity?—has let us down.

FITTING IN

Reports

Has made a sound beginning
Strikes the right note:
Encouraging, but dull.
Don't give them anything
To take hold of. Even
Pronouns are dangerous.

The good have no history,
So don't bother. *Satisfactory*
Should satisfy them.

Fair and *Quite good*,
Multi-purpose terms,
By meaning nothing,
Apply to all.
Feel free to deploy them.

Be on your guard;
Unmanageable oaf cuts both ways.
Finds the subject difficult,
Acquitting you, converts
Oaf into idiot, usher to master.

Parent, child, head,
Unholy trinity, will read
Your scripture backwards.
Set them no riddles, just
Echo the common-room cliché:
Must make more effort.

Remember your high calling:
School is the world.
Born at *Sound beginning*,
We move from *Satisfactory*
To *Fair*, then *Find*
The subject difficult,

Learning at last we
Could have done better.

Stone only, final instructor,
Modulates from the indicative
With *Rest in peace.*

Half-term

Always autumn, in my memory.
Butter ringing the drilled teashop crumpets;
Handmade chocolates, rich enough to choke you,
Brought in special smooth paper from Town.

(Back at school, the square tall piles
Of bread, featureless red jam in basins,
Grace, a shuffle of chairs, the separate table
For the visiting lacrosse team.)

Long awkward afternoons in hotel lounges,
Islanded in swollen armchairs, eyeing
Aristocratic horses in irrelevant magazines.
Should I be talking to Them?

(Back at school the raptly selfish
Snatch at self: the clashing
Determined duets in cold practising-
Rooms, the passionate solitary knitting.)

Inadequacies of presentation, perceived
By parents' temporary friends; hair, manners,
Clothes, have failed to adjust.
I don't know the rules of snooker.

(Back at school, the stiff reliable
Awkwardnesses of work. History test
On Monday morning. Deponent verbs.
I have never been good at maths.)

Saying goodbye. There are tears
And hugs, relief, regret. They,
Like me, return to a patterned life
Whose rules are easy. Unworthily

I shall miss chocolate, crumpets,
Comfort, but not the love I only
Sense as they go, waving to the end,
Vague in the streetlamps of November.

(Back at school the bullies,
Tyrants and lunatics are waiting.
I can deal with them.)

You will be hearing from us shortly

You feel adequate to the demands of this position?
What qualities do you feel you
Personally have to offer?

Ah

Let us consider your application form.
Your qualifications, though impressive, are
Not, we must admit, precisely what
We had in mind. Would you care
To defend their relevance?

Indeed

Now your age. Perhaps you feel able
To make your own comment about that,
Too? We are conscious ourselves
Of the need for a candidate with precisely
The right degree of immaturity.

So glad we agree

And now a delicate matter: your looks.
You do appreciate this work involves
Contact with the actual public? Might they,
Perhaps, find your appearance
Disturbing?

Quite so

And your accent. That is the way
You have always spoken, is it? What
Of your education? Were
You educated? We mean, of course,
Where were you educated?
And how
Much of a handicap is that to you,

Would you say?
Married, children,
We see. The usual dubious
Desire to perpetuate what had better
Not have happened at all. We do not
Ask what domestic disasters shimmer
Behind that vaguely unsuitable address.

And you were born—?

Yes. Pity.

So glad we agree.

Growing Out

We enter empty-handed, empty-hearted,
Freckled only by chromosomes and genes,
Novice-naked
(*Born on Monday*)

World, busy gossip, bustles up
Furnishing parents, a name,
A place in the sun
(*Christened on Tuesday*)

Parents erratically bombard us
With gifts—a rattle, love,
Uncles, words—tucking us in
To their particular nook.

The first growing out
Is easy. Bones shoot,
Teeth fall, appetites alter.
Parents officiate for us,
Handing down, or retailing
Through the columns of local papers.

Sometimes, if asked properly, they will
Deal with outmoded friends.

Growing out of parents
Is more expensive. Things
Of unquestioned presence—
A bed, a kettle, space—
Are suddenly unreliable;
They cost money.

We may also find we need
Someone to share them with
(*Married on Wednesday*)

These things, outgrown, become
Recriminatory. Best to consult
A specialist in division,
Who will slice accurately
Whatever is divisible:
House, money, children
(*Ill on Thursday*)

Finally we outgrow
Ourselves. Teeth and hair,
Being deciduous, drop;
Bones buckle and break;
Mind turns anarchist, body
Defects. Before long
We have grown out of everything
(*Worse on Friday*)

Free those who love you,
If you can, from posthumous
Distribution. Avoid
A cluttered end. Give
To the proper heirs before you go,
And celebrate your surrender
(*Died on Saturday*)

Grown out of all, you are now
Grown up. Empty-handed,
Empty-hearted, you have nothing
To hold you back
(*Buried on Sunday*)

Are ready to grow.

ONLY HERE FOR THE BIER

'I wrote these four poems because I was interested to see how the masculine world of Shakespeare's tragedies would look from the woman's angle. In fact, women exist in this world only to be killed, as sacrificial victims. So I imagined Gertrude (Mother-in-law), Regan (King's daughter), Emilia (Army wife) and the un-named waiting gentlewoman in *Macbeth* having a chat with some usual female confidante, like a hairdresser, or a telephone.'—U.A.F.

Mother-in-law

Such a nice girl. Just what I wanted
For the boy. Not top drawer, you know,
But so often, in our position, that
Turns out to be a mistake. They get
The ideas of their station, and that upsets
So many applecarts. The lieges, of course,
Are particularly hidebound, and the boy,
For all his absentminded ways, is a great one
For convention. Court mourning, you know . . .
Things like that. We don't want a Brunhilde
Here. But she was so suitable. Devoted
To her father and brother, and,
Of course, to the boy. And a very
Respectable, loyal family. Well, loyal
To number two, at any rate. Number one,
I remember, never quite trusted . . . Yes,
And had just the right interests. Folk song, for instance,
(Such a sweet little voice), and amateur
Dramatics. Inherited *that* taste
From her father. Dear old fellow, he'd go on
For hours about his college drama group.
And the boy's so keen on the stage. It's nice
When husband and wife have a shared interest,
Don't you think? Then botany. Poor little soul,
She was really keen. We'd go for trips
With the vasculum, and have such fun
Asking the lieges their country names for flowers.
Some of them, my dear, were scarcely delicate
(The names, I mean), but the young nowadays
Don't seem to notice. Marriage
Would have made her more innocent, of course.
I can't think who will do for the boy now.
I seem to be the only woman left round here.

King's daughter

Being the middle sister is tiresome.
The rawboned heroics of the eldest
Are out of reach; so is the youngest's
Gamine appeal. It is impossible for the second child
To be special. One must just cultivate
One's own garden, neatly. For neatness and order
Matter in the world of the middle daughter,
The even number. Disorderly lives
Are distasteful. Adultery is untidy;
Servants should be accurate and invisible.
Individuals should have two eyes, or none;
One eye is unacceptable. I enjoy the beauty
Of formality, and have no objection
To offering father the elaborate rhetoric
He expects. There is a certain correctness
In the situation. One must object, however,
To the impropriety of those who propose
Different rules. One is no innovator:
Innovation is unfeminine. It is important
That ashtrays should be emptied, and always
In the same place, that meals be punctual.
One depends on one's servants to supply
Visual and temporal symmetry. Equally,
One relies on one's family to support
The proper structure of relationships. It is a pity
That one's father is so eccentric, that his friends
Are the sort of people one tries not to know,
That one's sisters are, in their different ways,
Both so unwomanly. One would never dream
Of asserting onself in public, as they do.
One tries to cultivate the woman's touch.

Army wife

It's the place, I think. Everyone seems
To have gone to pieces here. Oh, not me,
My dear. I'm so used to the life. Just
Dump me down anywhere, and I'd make
A go of it—with reasonable living quarters,
Mind you, and good native servants.
Can't do without them! No, I don't count myself,
Nor Jim, of course. Jim keeps his cool
Whatever happens. We're old campaigners.
But take Mike. Such an awfully nice chap.
The new sort of officer, has a degree,
Staff College, all that sort of thing,
But absolutely no side. We think the world
Of Mike. So what does the silly ass do
But get himself mixed up with a native tart
(Very flashy girl—you've probably seen her around),
And a drunk-and-disorderly, and—oh, it's too shaming.
What the locals must be thinking! Mind you,
I blame the CO for all this. I know he's brilliant
In the field, but he *isn't* one of us, whatever
They may say. What's bred in the bone . . .
And somehow, here he's more noticeable.
There was that dreadful scene he made yesterday
About the laundry, and goodness knows
He ought to leave things like that
To his batman. Keeps a sword in his wardrobe,
They tell me. Yes, extraordinary, isn't it? A bit—
Well—*native*. And dear little Mrs CO—
Yes, isn't she a darling? Terribly good family,
But absolutely no side—she really has no idea
How to cope. I said to Jim, the trouble with you boys
Is, you need an enemy. Now the Wogs
Have packed up and gone home, you've simply
Nothing to do, so you get into trouble.
But Jim'll be all right. Jim keeps his cool
Whatever happens.

Waiting gentlewoman

If Daddy had known the setup,
I'm absolutely positive, he'd never
Have let me come. Honestly,
The whole thing's too gruesome
For words. There's nobody here to talk to
At all. Well, nobody under about ninety,
I mean. All the possible men have buggered
Off to the other side, and the rest,
Poor old dears, they'd have buggered off
Too, if their poor old legs would have
Carried them. HM's a super person, of course,
But she's a bit seedy just now,
Quite different from how marvellous she was
At the Coronation. And this doctor they've got in—
Well, he's only an ordinary little GP,
With a very odd accent, and even I
Can see that what HM needs is
A real psychiatrist. I mean, all this
About *blood*, and *washing*. Definitely Freudian.
As for Himself, well, definitely
Not my type. Daddy's got this thing
About selfmade men, of course, that's why
He was keen for me to come. But I think
He's gruesome. What HM sees in him
I cannot imagine. *And* he talks to himself.
That's so rude, I always think.
I hope Daddy comes for me soon.

CHRISTMAS CARDS

Angels' song

Intimates of heaven,
This is strange to us,
The unangelic muddle,
The birth, the human fuss.

We sing a harder carol now;
Holy the donkey in the hay;
Holy the manger made of wood,
Holy the nails, the blood, the clay.

BC:AD

This was the moment when Before
Turned into After, and the future's
Uninvented timekeepers presented arms.

This was the moment when nothing
Happened. Only dull peace
Sprawled boringly over the earth.

This was the moment when even energetic Romans
Could find nothing better to do
Than counting heads in remote provinces.

And this was the moment
When a few farm workers and three
Members of an obscure Persian sect

Walked haphazard by starlight straight
Into the kingdom of heaven.

Robin's Round

I am the proper
Bird for this season—
Not blessed St. Turkey,
Born to be eaten.

I'm man's incdible
Permanent bird.
I dine in his garden,
My spoon is his spade.

I'm the true token
Of Christ the Child-King:
I nest in man's stable,
I eat at man's table,
Through all his dark winters
I sing.

Reindeer Report

Chimneys: colder.
Flightpaths: busier.
Driver: Christmas (F)
Still baffled by postcodes.

Children: more
And stay up later.
Presents: heavier.
Pay: frozen.

Mission in spite
Of all this
Accomplished:

MERRY CHRISTMAS

The Contributors

Not your fault, gentlemen.
We acquit you of the calculatedly
Equivalent gift, the tinsel token.
Mary, maybe, fancied something more practical:
A layette, or at least a premium bond.
Firmly you gave the extravagantly
Useless, your present the unwrapped
Hard-edged stigma of vocation.

Not your fault, beasts,
Who donated your helpless animal
Rectitude to the occasion.
Not yours the message of the goblin
Robin, the red-nosed reindeer,
Nor had you in mind the yearly
Massacre of the poultry innocent,
Whom we judge correct for the feast.

Not your fault, Virgin,
Muddling along in the manger,
With your confused old man,
Your bastard baby, in conditions
No social worker could possibly approve.
How could your improvised, improvident
Holiness predict our unholy family Xmas,
Our lonely overdoses, deepfrozen bonhomie?

THE LIE OF THE LAND

On Buying OS sheet 163

I own all this. Not loutish acres
That tax the spirit, but the hawking
Eye's freehold, paper country.

Thirtytwo inches of aqueduct,
Windmill (disused), club house, embankment,
Public conveniences

In rural areas. This is my
Landlocked landscape that lives in cipher,
And is truer than walking.

Red and imperial, the Romans
Stride eastward. Mysterious, yellow,
The Salt Way halts and is gone.

Here, bigger than the hamlets they are,
Wild wayside syllables stand blooming:
Filkins, Lechlade, Broughton Poggs.

Here only I discard the umber
Reticulations of sad cities,
The pull and drag of mud.

Princetown

In the town it seems just a local
Joke, like piskies or Uncle Tom Cobley,
Though in rather poor taste. Souvenir mugs
Insistent as fat-bottomed mums on seaside postcards,
And tiny priapic men: *Property*
Of HM Prison, Dartmoor.
Not to be taken away. But if you walk
The ripped-up railway, its stonework
The patient, perfect carving of cheap labour,
To the quarries, you begin to imagine
The bald, tanned pates, grotesque livery,
Automatic warders, routine hopelessness,
But far off, historic, like walking
The Roman Wall, reconstructing
A massive alert garrison from piles
Of rubbish. So here, until, nearing the town,
We saw the discreet bulk, shining in twilight,
Each window equally watted. And I remembered
The mother and daughter, arm in arm and crying,
Outside the cafe offering cream teas.

At Cadbury

The knights keep the mound.
The native cattle, with their slow
Honourable look. Saracen swallows,
Bending argent and gules as they swoop,
Their winged scimitars slashing
The impassive air.

A young rabbit, too,
By the blackberries, with the same
White badge, clearly comic page to somebody.
Him I nearly caught. But the bird,
Unidentified, hawkish, that flew off, was master
Of the incident.

Where men didn't come.
Tennyson over Severn in laurelled Caerleon,
Sir Thomas in Newgate (whom God
Send good deliverance), and later White,
Dulling Irish exile with a red setter
And the DNB.

No need to come here.
Camelot towers' pennons wave anywhere.
This is simple Cadbury, on whose banks,
Nettled, cowpatted, introspection
Is impossible. You have to look out, to
The Apple Island,

Whose weird finger draws
Over twelve miles of commonplace Somerset
Magic conclusions. Arthur, perhaps,
Or somebody, looked out too,
At the grave of his long bones,
Which were not buried,

Though resurrected.
To come is to believe too much,
Or nothing. For here the unassertive landscape,
The web of sky, invisible fixed stars,
Braced in significance, discharge on us
Their need to doubt.

Hang-gliders in January

(*for C.K.*)

Like all miracles, it has a rational
Explanation; and like all miracles, insists
On being miraculous. We toiled
In the old car up from the lacklustre valley,
Taking the dogs because somebody had to,
At the heel of a winter Sunday afternoon

Into a sky of shapes flying:
Pot-bellied, shipless sails, dragonflies towering
Still with motion, daytime enormous bats,
Titanic tropical fish, and men,
When we looked, men strapped to wings,
Men wearing wings, men flying

Over a landscape too emphatic
To be understood: humdrum fields
With hedges and grass, the mythical river,
Beyond it the forest, the foreign high country.
The exact sun, navigating downwards
To end the revels, and you, and me,
The dogs, even, enjoying a scamper,
Avoiding scuffles.

It was all quite simple, really. We saw
The aground flyers, their casques and belts
And defenceless legs; we saw the earthed wings
Being folded like towels; we saw
The sheepskin-coated wives and mothers
Loyally watching; we saw a known,
Explored landscape by sunset-light,

We saw for ourselves how it was done,
From takeoff to landing. But nothing cancelled
The cipher of the soaring, crucified men,
Which we couldn't unravel; which gave us
Also, somehow, the freedom of air. Not
In vast caravels, triumphs of engineering,
But as men always wanted, simply,
Like a bird at home in the sky.

In The English Faculty Library, Oxford

(*for R.K.M.*)

It is a house of stairs. Books strain
Alphabetically upwards. Critics sprang
To eminence on their pages, and these bowed
Figures muse of vaulting after,
Through duly attested up-gradings
To doctorates. Beneath the spires
The academics dream.

It is a house of light. Technology
Illumines the dark reading, the blurred word.
With perfect vision, the bright-haired
(At sea with their sex-lives, finances,
Their futures, their tutors, sentenced
To match next essay with surly text)
Pelt down the feint tracks of dead game.

It is a house of peace. Gentle-
footed librarians pace the precincts.
Owen's legacy lies quiet. Sotto voce
Students make assignations and jokes; softly
They sharpen their pencils; inaudibly biros
Utter the last judgment.

It is a charnelhouse. The untongued dead
Wince at the touch of the lucky living.

It is a charnelhouse. The quick and young
Choke on the breath of refractory clay.

Down in the cellars the dead men grumble
Resenting, resisting the patterns
We make of their bones.

Haunted House

At six the furniture begins to fade.
Slit trenches' mouths gleam stickily along
The Axminster. Fixed bayonets look out
From cupboards. Gas and cordite tinge the air.
Hats turn to helmets as they hang. Outside
Hillocks of quicklime wait to hold the dead.

Children don't find this house by chance. A brown
Obsequious mongrel bitch seduces them
Into the magic garden, where faint smoke
Curls round the lily leaves. The oriole,
Night heron, bustard, bee-eater, composed
And friendly, eye their visitors with grace
And never move away. Strange trees extend
Embroidered hands. The air purrs with desire.

This stair promises something. Painted heads
Smile in its angles. Glowing shoulders, lace,
Arms, ringlets, sapphires, eyes, attest some force.
Concealed among the bosoms, spiky heads
Of Samurai, speared, tiger-whiskered, peer
In search of enemies twin to themselves.

At last, the lady and her room. Tea waits;
Smart bread-and-butter; polished brandysnaps;
Hands patrol teacups; angel cake presides;
Gentleman's relish sounds a richer note.
The children eat and drink. The day grows dark.
At six the furniture begins to fade.

Rural Guerillas

The dead sticks of winter rise in their graves.
The future pokes through them, exploding
Like pointillist grapeshot.

Landroving weeds lay jagged boobytraps.
Young daffodils rear ponderous heads
The shape of torpedoes.

Along the hedgerows impatient snipers
Pepper the air with their random bright
Volleys, declaring green.

The shouts and stutters and shamefaced mumbles
Of garden birds: recruits rehearsing
The trenches' foul language.

In the air, incorrigible Cockney
Thumbs-up of chestnut buds, embarking
For the spring offensive.

Under the tarmac the depth charge daisies
Brace knees and shoulders for the moment
When they hijack the world.

GODS & MORTALS

Getting it across

(for Caroline)

'His disciples said unto him, Lo, now speakest thou plainly, and speakest no proverb. Now are we sure that thou knowest all things.'
St John, ch. 16, vv. 29–30.

This is the hard thing.
Not being God, the Son of Man,
—I was born for that part—
But patiently incising on these yokel faces,
Mystified, bored and mortal,
The vital mnemonics they never remember.

There is enough of Man in my God
For me to construe their frowns. I feel
The jaw-cracking yawns they try to hide
When out I come with one of my old
Chestnuts. *Christ! not that bloody*
Sower again, they are saying, or *God!*
Not the Prodigal fucking Son.
Give us a new one, for Messiah's sake.

They know my unknowable parables as well
As each other's shaggy dog stories.
I say! I say! I say! There was this Samaritan,
This Philistine and this Roman . . . or
What did the high priest say
To the belly dancer? All they need
Is the cue for laughs. My sheep and goats,
Virgins, pigs, figtrees, loaves and lepers
Confuse them. Fishing, whether for fish or men,
Has unfitted them for analogy.

Yet these are my mouths. Through them only
Can I speak with Augustine, Aquinas, Martin, Paul,
Regius Professors of Divinity,
And you, and you.

How can I cram the sense of Heaven's kingdom
Into our pidgin-Aramaic quayside jargon?

I envy Moses, who could choose
The diuturnity of stone for waymarks
Between man and Me. He broke the tablets,
Of course. I too know the easy messages
Are the ones not worth transmitting;
But he could at least carve.
The prophets too, however luckless
Their lives and instructions, inscribed on wood,
Papyrus, walls, their jaundiced oracles.

I alone must write on flesh. Not even
The congenial face of my Baptist cousin,
My crooked affinity Judas, who understands,
Men who would give me accurately to the unborn
As if I were something simple, like bread.
But Pete, with his headband stuffed with fishhooks,
His gift for rushing in where angels wouldn't,
Tom, for whom metaphor is anathema,
And James and John, who want the room at the top—
These numskulls are my medium. I called them.

I am tattooing God on their makeshift lives.
My Keystone Cops of disciples, always
Running absurdly away, or lying ineptly,
Cutting off ears and falling into the water,
These Sancho Panzas must tread my Quixote life,
Dying ridiculous and undignified,
Flayed and stoned and crucified upside down.
They are the dear, the human, the dense, for whom
My message is. That might, had I not touched them,
Have died decent respectable upright deaths in bed.

Pomona and Vertumnus

Lady of kitchen-gardens, learned
In the ways of the early thin-skinned rhubarb,
Whose fingers fondle each gooseberry bristle,
Stout currants sagging on their flimsy stalks,
And sprinting strawberries, that colonise
As quick as Rome.

Goddess of verges, whose methodical
Tenderness fosters the vagrant croppers,
Gawky raspberry refugees from gardens,
Hip, sloe, juniper, blackberry, crab,
Humble abundance of heath, hedge, copse,
The layabouts' harvest.

Patron of orchards, pedantic observer
Of rites, of prune, graft, spray and pick,
In whose honour the Bramleys' branches
Bow with their burly cargo, from grass-deep
To beyond ladders; you who teach pears their proper shape,
And brush the ripe plum's tip with a touch of crystal.

I know your lovers, earth's grubby godlings:
Silvanus, whose province is muck-heaps
And electric fences; yaffle-headed Picus;
Faunus the goatman. All of them friends
Of the mud-caked cattle, courting you gruffly
With awkward, touching gifts.

But I am the irrepressible, irresponsible
Spirit of Now: no constant past,
No predictable future. All my genius
Goes into moments. I have nothing to give
But contradiction and alteration.

Me, therefore, the wise goddess picked
When I came to her, true to my bent,
In the form of an old woman.

Janus

I am the two-headed anniversary god,
Lord of the Lupercal and the Letts diary.
I have a head for figures.

My clocks are the moon and sun,
My almanac the zodiac. The ticktock seasons,
The hushabye seas are under my thumb.

From All Saints to All Souls I celebrate
The da capo year. My emblems are albums,
The bride's mother's orchid corsage, the dark cortège.

Master of the silent passacaglia
Of the future, I observe the dancers,
But never teach them the step.

I am the birthday prescience
Who knows the obituary, the tombstone's arithmetic.
Not telling is my present.

I monitor love through its mutations
From paper to ruby. I am archivist
Of the last divorce and the first kiss.

I am director of the forgotten fiesta.
I know why men at Bacup black their faces;
Who horned at Abbots Bromley tread the mazes.

I am the future's overseer, the past's master.
See all, know all, speak not.
I am the two-faced god.

Genesis

(for J. R. R. Tolkien)

In the beginning were the words,
Aristocratic, cryptic, chromatic.
Vowels as direct as mid-day,
Consonants lanky as long-swords.

Mouths materialised to speak the words:
Leafshaped lips for the high language,
Tranquil tongues for the tree-creatures,
Slits and slobbers for the lower orders.

Deeds came next, words' children.
Legs by walking evolved a landscape.
Continents and chronologies occurred,
Complex and casual as an implication.

Arched over all, alarming nimbus,
Magic's disorderly thunder and lightning.

The sage sat in his suburban fastness,
Garrisoned against progress. He grieved
At what the Duke's men did to our words
(Whose war memorial is every signpost).

The sage sat. And middle-earth
Rose around him like a rumour.
Grave grammarians, Grimm and Verner,
Gave it laws, granted it charters.

The sage sat. But the ghosts walked
Of the Birmingham schoolboy, the Somme soldier,
Whose bones lay under the hobbit burrows,
Who endured darkness, and friends dying,

Whom words waylaid in a Snow Hill siding,
Coal truck pit names, grimy, gracious,
Blaen-Rhondda, *Nantyglo*, *Senghenydd*.
In these deeps middle-earth was mined.

These were the words in the beginning.

Chorus

We are here to bear witness.
We would much rather be somewhere else.
We are not necessary.

We stand on suburban carpets, we sit
On three-piece suites of uncut moquette,
Under the detached retina of television.
Summoned to bear witness, we attend.
We do not understand our part.

Inexorably on our thin inexperienced
Shoulders the stiff vestments descend.
Head and hand assume the dragging
Gestures of hierophants. Our bodies assent
To the ceremony. We have become The Chorus.

But this is absurd! We're not in a play.
In our world, this is the hour
For winding clocks, walking dogs, cleaning teeth.
We have embarrassing little needs. I should like
To go to the lavatory; to look at my watch; to yawn.

The protagonist has the gift of tongues,
The hurt heart will spurt words all night.
We know the future, but we must not say so.
Our part is to bear witness. This is not our play.
We are not expected to interfere.

We are not necessary, but we are needed.
We sit, stand, speak, are silent,
Responding to archaic, unexpected promptings
We are too polite to defy. In the satyr play
Tomorrow, how we shall burlesque all this!

Father in the Railway Buffet

What are you doing here, ghost, among these urns,
These film-wrapped sandwiches and help-yourself biscuits,
Upright and grand, with your stick, hat and gloves,
Your breath of eau-de-cologne?

What have you to say to these head-scarfed tea-ladies,
For whom your expensive vowels are exotic as Japan?
Stay, ghost, in your proper haunts, the clubland smokerooms,
Where you know the waiters by name.

You have no place among these damp and nameless.
Why do you walk here? *I came to say goodbye.*
You were ashamed of me for being different.
It didn't matter.

You who never even learned to queue?

Birthday Poem

'Here come two noble beasts in, a man and a lion.'

Conscientious; a quiet man,
Not helped by the naïve histrionics
Of Bottom, the adolescent tantrums
Of fluffy-chinned Flute.

A diffident reader; anxious
About his limitations; keen
To embark on the difficult labour
Of learning the cues for roaring.

Honest as sunlight
He stands before the giggling
Intelligentsia, disclaiming illusion.
They must not suppose he is
What he is not. He is just
A man as other men are.

His careful confession made,
Unlike poor knock-kneed Moonshine,
Capitulating to high-bred heckling,
He does his job properly,
Like the master-craftsman he is.

The lion performs his pantomime part:
He roars; he tears Thisbe's cloak.
Well roared, Lion! He thinks
His sedulous hours of rehearsing
Munificently tipped, being himself
Too candid to know irony.

This for you, Leo, whose lion likewise
Is *a very gentle beast*
And of a good conscience.

You share his carpenter's
Steadfast standards, intelligent fingers,
Joy in making. Even his name,
With all its subharmonics, defines
Precisely you: lion among ladies,
The joiner, Snug.

The Colourblind Birdwatcher

In sallow summer
The loud-mouthed birds
Peer through my hedges
As brown as swallows.

In acrid autumn
High-flying birds
Splay in formation
As brown as magpies.

In the wan winter
Audacious birds
Besiege my windows
As brown as robins.

In sepia spring
The punctual birds
Resume their habits
As brown as blossom.

95

Three storeys up, she lives under the eaves
In the sky's suburbs. From above
She knows the tabby shoulders of pigeons,
The painted hair of men.

Downstairs is another country, its frontier
A childgate. On slippered, uncertain feet,
Armed with a Zimmer, she mans
The landing, her treacherous border.

Goliath voices intone in her
Diminishing kingdom, declaiming the weather's
Intentions, the future's enormous transactions.
Her armchair's horizon is global.

In it she waits for her tiny Doomsday.
Her drawers are tidied for good, and then
Untidied again. Life keeps on being picked up,
Like a tedious piece of knitting.

So she idles out her epilogue
In her eyrie, looking down upon living
As a small, difficult theorem
She could solve once. And in her windows

Her small, difficult plants turning sunwards
Obstinately, perpetually flower.

Child in Marble

Here lie I, 'little Julia',
Interred between inverted commas
Like a dead canary.

I alone know who I was, what
I would have done. For my parents
My lack of finish completes me.

I am their emblem of precocious
Mortality. They remember my passing,
My meningeal convulsions, my spasmodic screaming,

The trained nurse, the little frilly frocks
Quickly given away after, the unpredictable
Silences and weeping.

Under my green grave chippings
I repudiate my axiomatic pathos.
I am not just a dead baby,

Undistinguishable in albums from
My ringletted, be-smocked siblings,
Eponyms of childhood, so similar

That no one now knows who was which.
Under the secretive façade of childhood
I grasped the blueprint of my own definition.

They have sterilised me in the fires
Of my dying, and concluded me.
But I was the future I missed,

My revised version of childhood,
My histrionic adolescence, my flowering
Into brains and graces, my marriages,

My children, ungrown because of my going,
My implicit, uncompromised self, my dark corners.
I claim to have been me, not

What they remember, their child,
Formal and meaningless as a marble cherub,
Signalling mourning by an empty urn.

Portraits of Tudor Statesmen

Surviving is keeping your eyes open,
Controlling the twitchy apparatus
Of iris, white, cornea, lash and lid.

So the literal painter set it down—
The sharp raptorial look; strained eyeball;
And mail, ruff, bands, beard, anything, to hide
The violently vulnerable neck.

CALLED UP

The Constant Tin Soldier

I. BREAKING DAY

Dying is easier.
Just a flick of somebody's finger,
Then the icy exactness of rigor mortis,
While posthumous flies and decorations settle,
A subaltern writes thirty-two letters
By torchlight to next of kin,
And the Germans advance in your boots,
Which are better than theirs.

It isn't always lucky to stay alive.
Some never recover from surviving.
The showy heraldry of scars excuses,
But not the chronic tic of terror,
Picked up on a foggy March morning
Between the Staffords and the Suffolks,
Between Bullecourt and Croisilles.
You will carry this day like a tumour
In your head for life, fusilier,
And no one will ever needle it out.

You remember the date:

21st March, 1918. Day
Of the Kaiserschlacht, day
Of the German Spring Offensive.
We, the beaten, have no name for that day
In our own language.

Your remember your place:

Third Army, 34th Division,
102nd brigade. HQ Gomiecourt
(Which I never saw) under
Lt Col Charlton (whom I never

Saw again after. Only now, sixty years on,
A youngster tells me he was taken prisoner.
I thought him killed).
23rd Northumberland Fusiliers.

You remember the weather:

Sun on the 20th, following rain
And squally winds. Enemy weathermen
Prophesied continuing calm. It would be safe,
They said, to use gas against us. Then
An intense, still morning; no wind;
But ground mist ghosting
To dense, inimical fog.

Your remember the timing:

0440 hours: artillery bombardment begins.
Five hours of General Surprise Fire.
The German brass, guns, mortars and howitzers,
Jarring in unison. It rained noise,
Mud, bone, hot lumps of jagged metal,
Gas, smoke, fear, darkness, dissolution
By the clock, if any clock ticked on.
0940 hours: infantry attack begins,
Across the broken earth, the broken men.
An orderly advance; they sauntered
Over the unstrung landscape.

You remember your state:

Fear, fog, solitude,
Between Bullecourt and Croisilles,
Between the Staffords and the Suffolks.
We had to man the Forward Zone,
But creeping with the creeping fog
Came in the enemy. We knew them
By the shape of their helmets. They were
Where we were. Nothing was where
It had been on the map, and no one

Was one of us. The counties melted,
And their quiet local voices. My friend
Died, I was on my own.

Your remember your mood:

Orphaned. The formal beauty
Of rank, its cordial courteous bearing,
Had foundered. No one to give
Or receive orders. Our training
Was scrappy; we had never studied
The delicate art of retreat, and our trumpets
Had mud in their throats.

You remember your choice:

Flight. Through craters, corpses,
Stumps of horses, guns and trees,
Through fog and my everyman darkness.
What are the rules for the solitary
Soldier? Should he stand firm
To the last pointless volley,
Or lay down his arms at the feet
Of kind enemies, and be whisked
By their finished techniques
To a snug internment? No one
Had drilled enterprise into us.
Choice had been frightened to death.
I could do only what I did,
What the primitive man I muzzle
Inside me made me do: I ran.

You remember the sequel:

Rehabilitation. The comfort of being
Among confederates, men
Who had hobbled their way back, stubbornly,
Without heroism. Most of us still
Had our uses. Mine was liaison

With American troops. Gigantic,
Buoyant, ignorant, they trod
Our shellshocked fief, as once their ancestors
Trampled across the New World.
I guided them along the labyrinths,
Interpreted, explained, a ghost of war,
Leading the living down the dead men's trenches.

You remember your self:

I had archaic longings,
Yearned for the dead and the lost,
The officers, the other ranks, the men
I belonged with, who knew the same songs,
Shouted on United. Not even
Graves for most, just Memorials
To the Missing. I missed them,
All the canny Geordie lads
With their feet still through the night
And the days.

2. SPOILS OF PEACE

Some of the dead were signallers:
Rupert the Fair and Wilfred the Wise,
Isaac the exile and innocent Ivor,
And Edward, who endured.

In various ways, these died,
And so, afterwards, in some ways,
Some of the living perhaps listened.

The dead can afford to be generous,
Having no superannuation rights.
These men squandered the spoils of war,
But I latched on to my red-edged learning,

Investing sensibly in job, house, car,
Wife and children, dog and skivvy.
Redoubts and outworks, manned by me,
To balk the enemy at my back.

I couldn't afford to be taken
The same way twice; kept short accounts,
Checked the wiring, planted sharp roses,
Trained the dog to the qui vive.

But upkeep has to be paid for. I traded
My craftsman's hands for a salesman's pay.
Built my house on my tongue. Charm
Was the mortar, the brickwork cheek.

In a world fit for heroes, heroism
Is de trop. You have to fight
With guile for your rights, against
The agenda-adept, the minutes-men.

I mastered the means that made men mine,
Not shadows, to fade in the gassed thicket,
But beefy reliable cheque-signing fingers,
Dewlaps to dance at my bagman's patter.

I held the line, from Wallsend to Workington,
Where the Romans were, I came.
Chatted up waitresses, chaffed the barmen,
Sold my soul to keep myself safe.

(Not between Croisilles and Bullecourt.)

Good morning!
                                        Good gracious!
                                                                    Nice day.
                                                                                        Delightful.
Any tonics, tinctures or pick-me-ups?
No.
Thank you. I'll call again.
                                                        Good morning.
                                                                                    Nice day.

Where the wind whips over the fraying border,
Where homesick legions were whittled away,
On the frontier of failure I jobbed and prospered,
Natty, dapper, with my quickfire smile.

Not the dovetailed sockets, the tonguing and grooving,
The crisscross network I could have carved,
But a web of hardheaded sceptical buyers,
Whom I forced at jokepoint to be my friends.

Good morning!
                                        Good morning.
                                                                        Nice day.
                                                                                            Yes.
Any false rumours, horrors or hangovers?
No thank you.
I'll call again.
                                Do.
                                        Good morning.
                                                                        Good morning.
Shocking day.

Back at HQ the walls stood firm.
I saw to that. But the garrison
Could never be trusted. Maids
Came and went, children were born

And died. The dog too. I procured
Replacements, held weekly inspections,
Reviewed morale, kept up my payments,
Insured house, contents and livestock, checked

The defences. There was nothing amiss.
But somehow I had enlisted
A saboteur, not a friend (my friend
Died). She gave me nothing

To complain of; collaborated in all
Transactions, performed creditably
At trade functions, answered the telephone
Adequately. But I didn't like

The sort of book she read. Disaffection
Was plain in her children. The boy

A myopic coward, whose only solution
Was running away. Then the girl

Who died. I forget her name now,
But she cost me a mint of money
At the time, one way and the other.
As for the substitute, I recognised

A usurper in her. She'd have ousted
Me, taken my place if she could,
Mutinous, sulky, and damnably
Heir to my look and my hands.

I had carved out a kingdom
For my son to inherit. But he
Renegued, would have none of it,
Fancied his own improvident way,

Instead of cultivating my contacts.
Married a fatherless, unsuitable
Outspoken girl from down south somewhere,
Ran to the opposite end of the earth

And stayed there. Good riddance.
One less mouth to feed, one less craven
In the camp. The girl deserted too,
After a prolonged, costly education

Without a dividend. No hope there
Of a son-in-law, someone I could
Have trusted, canny chap, living close,
To keep an eye on the wiring, the blood-pressure,

Someone I could have taken to, without
That yellow streak in him. But I managed
Without. Anticipated the next assault
(Infirmity, loneliness, death) and took

Precautionary measures: transferred HQ
To a high-rise residence for the well-heeled,
Heated centrally, caretakered, with lift,
Where care would be taken.

Here we live now, annuitied. I ignore
The persistent trickle of offstage
Deaths, as my feebler contemporaries
Fall out. Life has taught me
To concentrate on living. This I do.

My primitive man is dead, crushed
By cordial years of cronies. I couldn't
Speak straight now if I tried.
I am the kerbside cheapjack's patter:

Ladies, watch what I do.
The genuine article. 20 pound in the catalogue,
18 in the shops, 15 in the sales. But from me—
Stand close, ladies—*a fiver!*
Ladies, watch what I do.

Watch, ladies, what I do.
Holidays abroad yearly, until age
Made us uninsurable. Now a five-star
Scottish hydro, where I am known

To the management. I am still standing to,
Between the Staffords and the Suffolks,
As I have been for most of my life.
I may be only a tin soldier,
But I have been constant.

Standing To

This is turning into a long war.
I must have been mobilised
In the womb. I know nothing
Of a prewar world. I ponder
The finicky distinctions of peace.

Service is secretive,
Camouflage always
Congenial. Medals
Have not been worn for years.

Martial paraphernalia—
Barrage balloons, fly-by-night signposts,
Rationing, passwords, internment,
The planes marked *Us* and *Them*—

Are the apparatus
Of children's games.

The enemy is not
The one who declares war,
Who is as mortal as you.

The true enemy declares
Nothing, cannot be disposed of,
Is never indisposed.

I was set here
To watch. So I do,
And report, in cipher, to headquarters,
Which is an hypothesis.

Are there others recruited
Like me, encoding what they see,
Abandoned by Higher Command,
Unable to desert?

Is the war perhaps over,
Mine an irrelevant garrison?

I doubt my calling, but still hear
The thin paper voices
From south-coast resorts
Reporting flak, then falling
Suddenly silent.